JUL 07 2014

BLUE BANNER
BIOGRAPHY

Drew
BREES

Pete DiPrimio

Mitchell Lane
PUBLISHERS

P.O. Box 196
Hockessin, Delaware 19707
Visit us on the web: www.mitchelllane.com
Comments? email us: mitchelllane@mitchelllane.com

Mitchell Lane
PUBLISHERS

Printing   2   3   4   5   6   7   8   9

Blue Banner Biographies

Alicia Keys	Gwen Stefani	Megan Fox
Allen Iverson	Ice Cube	Miguel Tejada
Ashanti	Jamie Foxx	Nancy Pelosi
Ashlee Simpson	Ja Rule	Natasha Bedingfield
Ashton Kutcher	Jay-Z	Orianthi
Avril Lavigne	Jennifer Lopez	Orlando Bloom
Beyoncé	Jessica Simpson	P. Diddy
Blake Lively	J. K. Rowling	Peyton Manning
Bow Wow	Joe Flacco	Pink
Brett Favre	John Legend	Queen Latifah
Britney Spears	Justin Berfield	Rihanna
Carrie Underwood	Justin Timberlake	Robert Downey Jr.
C.C. Sabathia	Kanye West	Robert Pattinson
Chris Brown	Kate Hudson	Ron Howard
Chris Daughtry	Katy Perry	Sean Kingston
Christina Aguilera	Keith Urban	Selena
Ciara	Kelly Clarkson	Shakira
Clay Aiken	Kenny Chesney	Shia LaBeouf
Cole Hamels	Kesha	Shontelle Layne
Condoleezza Rice	Kristen Stewart	Soulja Boy Tell 'Em
Corbin Bleu	Lady Gaga	Stephenie Meyer
Daniel Radcliffe	Lance Armstrong	Taylor Swift
David Ortiz	Leona Lewis	T.I.
David Wright	Lil Wayne	Timbaland
Derek Jeter	Lindsay Lohan	Tim McGraw
Drew Brees	Ludacris	Toby Keith
Eminem	Mariah Carey	Usher
Eve	Mario	Vanessa Anne Hudgens
Fergie	Mary J. Blige	Zac Efron
Flo Rida	Mary-Kate and Ashley Olsen	

Library of Congress Cataloging-in-Publication Data
DiPrimio, Pete.
  Drew Brees / by Pete DiPrimio.
     p. cm. — (Blue banner biographies)
  Includes bibliographical references and index.
  ISBN 978-1-58415-911-7 (library bound)
  1. Brees, Drew, 1979– — Juvenile literature. 2. Football players — United States — Biography — Juvenile literature. 3. Quarterbacks (Football) — United States — Biography — Juvenile literature. 4. New Orleans Saints (Football team) — Juvenile literature. I. Title.
  GV939.B695D57 2011
  796.332092 — dc22
  [B]
                                                                                      2010014889

ABOUT THE AUTHOR: Pete DiPrimio is an award-winning sports columnist for the *Fort Wayne* [Indiana] *News-Sentinel*, a longtime freelance feature, fiction, and travel writer. He covers college football, including Purdue, where Drew Brees starred. He is the author of three nonfiction books pertaining to Indiana University athletics, and of *Tom Brady, Eli Manning,* and *Ancient Rome* for Mitchell Lane Publishers. He graduated from Ball State University with honors, earning a Bachelor of Science degree with a minor in history. He lives in Bloomington, Indiana.

PUBLISHER'S NOTE: This book is based on the author's interviews with Joe Tiller, Tom Schott, and Matt Painter of the Purdue University Boilermakers. The story has been thoroughly researched, and to the best of our knowledge represents a true story. While every possible effort has been made to ensure accuracy, the publisher will not assume liability for damages caused by inaccuracies in the data and makes no warranty on the accuracy of the information contained herein. This story has not been authorized or endorsed by Drew Brees.

Blue Banner Biography

Drew Brees celebrates the New Orleans Saints' Super Bowl victory with son Baylen and wife Brittany.

Hero

Drew Brees couldn't stop the tears. He didn't want to. The New Orleans Saints quarterback had shredded one of the National Football League's fiercest defenses. In the biggest game of his life he had completed pass after pass, made play after play, and now came the biggest reward.

No, not the Super Bowl trophy for beating the Indianapolis Colts, although that was special.

No, not winning the Super Bowl MVP Award and earning a trip to Disney World to ride in a Magic Kingdom parade with Mickey Mouse, although that was cool.

No, not even having fans so thankful for all he had done for their team and their city that they had photos made of him walking on water. They called him "Breesus" in a twist on "Jesus" because Drew was, in many ways, their savior.

Drew's biggest moment at Sun Life Stadium in Miami came in the 31-17 victory celebration when he held his one-year-old son, Baylen Robert, high in the air as thousands of strips of white, blue, orange, and red confetti fell around them. He put headphones on Baylen to protect his ears from the loud noise of the roaring crowd and rocking music. He kissed his son's hands, hugged his wife, Brittany, and enjoyed living a dream.

All his life somebody had told him he was too short, too injured, too this and that to be a successful quarterback.

Not anymore.

In three playoff games, under the highest-possible pressure, Drew threw eight touchdowns and zero interceptions.

"I won't forget those people," he told Tim Layden of *Sports Illustrated*, "because they motivated me."

In Super Bowl XLIV, Drew faced Indianapolis' Peyton Manning, considered one of the greatest quarterbacks ever, and beat him. Manning had already won a Super Bowl plus a record four NFL Most Valuable Player awards. Drew had done none of those things, but he didn't blink.

It took him a quarter to calm down while Indianapolis jumped to a 10-0 lead. After that, Drew completed 29 of 32 passes (one of those passes was dropped, another was intentionally spiked to stop the clock), including his last 10. He finished 32-for-39 for 288 yards, two touchdowns, and a quarterback rating of 114.5 when 100.0 is considered exceptional. The 32 completions tied New England quarterback Tom Brady's Super Bowl record. The victory tied a Super Bowl record for greatest comeback.

This wasn't a fluke. In three playoff games, under the highest-possible pressure, Drew threw eight touchdowns and zero interceptions. In 2009 he set an NFL record for accuracy by completing 70.6 percent of his passes. Between 2004 and 2009 he made the Pro Bowl four times.

Not bad for a guy who was a backup to 38-year-old Doug Flutie as a rookie, who had a losing record as a starter after his first two seasons, and who four years earlier was unwanted by nearly every team in the league.

Did Drew's former college coach at Purdue University, Joe Tiller, see this coming?

"I don't want to suggest I had a crystal ball," Tiller said, "but nothing Drew does surprises me. He's very talented. He was underrated by the professional people when he came out. What I witnessed him do at the college level was amazing.

"Not only has Drew matured into a real field general, but he's with a coach who knows what his strengths are. This system complements him perfectly."

Drew has big hands, which helps him control the ball. He also has good footwork. As funny as it sounds, being a good quarterback starts with your feet. The better your footwork, which means staying balanced and lined up correctly, the more accurately and the harder you throw. Drew benefitted from years of playing tennis, which also demands good footwork.

"Nothing Drew does surprises me. He's very talented. . . . What I witnessed him do at the college level was amazing."

It helps that Drew is a very good athlete. During a dramatic comeback victory over Miami in 2009, Drew ran for a touchdown, then got so excited that he dunked the football over the goalpost, which is 10 feet high. Not bad for a guy barely 6 feet tall. Teammates joked that he used an elevator, a ladder, a springboard, and a player's back to get that high.

The Saints were once so bad, fans wore bags over their heads because they didn't want people to know who they were. They were 3-13 the year before Drew Brees arrived. In four years he led them to a Super Bowl victory.

"Drew is an amazing athlete," New Orleans coach Sean Payton said during the press conference after the Super Bowl. "His foot speed and ball location, those traits are rare. I think that probably is a little underrated with him."

Why is Drew so good? Payton said it's because of how hard Drew works. The coach told a story of one Sunday, when the Saints had a bye week and didn't play, he was leaving the team practice building and saw Brees by himself on the practice field. Payton asked his quarterback what he was doing. Drew said he was trying to stay in his routine and simulate a game so that his body would stay in condition.

Drew once gave Payton a book called *212: The Extra Degree*. Why? At 211 degrees, water is just really hot. At 212, it boils. That's how much just one more degree means. Drew's preparation is about doing enough to get that extra degree.

"He might have been the best practice player I've ever been around," Tiller said. "He was all business, and still is."

Although Drew is very serious, he can also have fun. How much fun?

"He's one of the few people I know who can recite every line from the movie *Caddyshack*," said Tom Schott, Purdue's assistant athletic director for sports information. "You could pick a line from any part of the movie and he could finish it."

Drew is still a teenager at heart. Ever since his high school days, he has led a pregame chant with his teammates. He changes it every year. The one he used for the 2009 season came from a trip he took to a U.S. military base at Guantanamo Bay in Cuba. He spent a morning doing physical training with Marines and picked up one of their chants, then changed it for the Saints. Here's the chant they used before the Super Bowl:

> One, two, win for you!
> Three, four, win some more!
> Five, six, win again!
> Seven, eight, win, great!
> Nine, ten, win again!
> Again, again, again, again!

The Saints did win. And New Orleans, famous for its parties and Mardi Gras, celebrated as never before.

If it weren't for Drew Brees, it would never have happened.

The Early Years

Drew was born on January 15, 1979, in Dallas, Texas, with a fuzzy brown birthmark on his right cheek. His parents, Chip and Mina, named him after Dallas Cowboys receiver Drew Pearson. Mina wondered if the birthmark was caused when she fell on her right side on an icy sidewalk just before delivery. "That's where an angel kissed you," she told him. The family considered surgery to remove it, then decided not to.

Drew has a brother, Reid, who is two years younger. His parents divorced when Drew was eight, a year after the family moved to Westlake, Texas.

Drew grew up playing sports. One of his best was tennis. He was good enough to be ranked as high as No. 3 in the nation in the twelve-year-old age group, good enough to beat future tennis pro and U.S. Open champion Andy Roddick three times before Drew gave up the sport at thirteen. However, he wasn't good enough to beat his mother (Mina played on the Austin city championship team and wanted him to stick with tennis), and that bothered him because he was so competitive.

Drew is one of the best athletes in the NFL. He once was a nationally ranked tennis player, and he's a good enough golfer to play in major celebrity tournaments.

Even today Drew wants to win in everything—golf, tennis, bowling, fishing.

Oh, yes. And in football.

Athleticism runs in Drew's family. His grandfather, Ray Akins, was a former Marine who became one of the most successful high school football coaches in Texas history. When he retired in 1988, Ray had 302 wins, the third-highest record in Texas. Mina played four sports in high school and was a baseball cheerleader at Texas A&M, where she met

Chip, who played a year of basketball there. One of Drew's uncles, Marty Akins, was an all–Southwest Conference quarterback at the University of Texas in 1975. Marty had played with Heisman Trophy winner and future NFL star Earl Campbell.

"What we liked about [Brees] was that he was a winner, he was accurate and he was smart."
-Coach Joe Tiller

Drew played football, basketball, and baseball at Westlake High School, but it was obvious football was his best sport. His heroes growing up were former NFL quarterbacks Joe Montana and Drew Bledsoe.

Drew started his last two years and led Westlake to a 28-0-1 record, including 16-0 and the Class 5A (biggest school) state title as a senior. He threw for 5,461 yards and 50 touchdowns in high school. That was good, but he tore a left knee ligament at the end of his junior year. That scared off Texas and Texas A&M, the schools he was interested in.

Not everyone was scared. Joe Tiller, the coach at the University of Wyoming, started recruiting Brees. The quarterback wasn't interested. When Tiller took the Purdue job, Brees became interested because the Purdue Boilermakers were in the Big Ten, one of the nation's best conferences.

"What we liked about him was that he was a winner, he was accurate and he was smart," Tiller said.

Drew's choices came down to Kentucky and Purdue. As it turned out, it wasn't a choice at all.

Hurricane Drew

Drew arrived with big dreams in West Lafayette in August of 1997. He was one of the best freshmen in the nation's 10th-ranked recruiting class. Then he ran into a big reality—he wasn't going to play much that first year. No matter. He would wait and learn and never, ever, let mistakes hold him back.

"When he threw an interception," Tiller said, "he thought those [jerks] were lucky to intercept it. He would quickly move on to the next play. You have to. If you're thinking about the last play, you'll never execute the next play."

Tiller's offense was so pass-friendly—it was called basketball on grass—that in his first year he turned a defensive back, Billy Dicken, into a star quarterback. Drew was a seldom-used backup. He was in line to become the starter as a sophomore, but Tiller wasn't sure if he was ready, so he signed a junior college quarterback

"We knew Drew was extremely accurate," Tiller said, "but we had no idea how he'd react in a game. He played some as a freshman and managed to hit the open linebacker several times."

Drew's arm made him a superstar at Purdue, but his feet often got him out of trouble.

It wasn't long before Drew was hitting his open receivers.

"Other teams have a progression ready where the quarterback will look at receiver 1, 2, 3," Tiller told Kevin Kaminski of *Football News*. "Drew finds receiver 5 and 6."

Drew put up eye-popping numbers as a sophomore in 1998. Against Minnesota he was 31-for-36 for 522 yards and six touchdowns in a 56-21 win. In a 31-24 loss at Wisconsin he set a national record with 83 passing attempts, and tied the record with 55 completions. Overall he set school records with 3,983 passing yards and 39 touchdowns. He was the Big Ten's offensive player of the year.

Nick Saban, then the Michigan State coach, said Drew's quick feet and accuracy reminded him of NFL Hall-of-Fame quarterback Joe Montana. People gave him nicknames like "Cool Brees" and "Hurricane Drew."

> *He reminded [Nick Saban] of NFL Hall-of-Fame quarterback Joe Montana. People gave him nicknames like "Cool Brees . . ."*

As a junior in 1999, Drew led Purdue to a 7-5 record and the Outback Bowl. He threw for 25 touchdowns against 12 interceptions. He finished fourth in voting for the Heisman Trophy, which is given every year to the nation's best player.

Drew rarely had free time. After afternoon practice he'd study for his classes in industrial management, calculus, economics, and physics. Around 11 P.M. he'd begin studying film of the next opponent. He did find time to meet Brittany, his future wife, the summer before his senior year. She was also a Purdue student.

Drew has always been a winner. His teams have won at every level.

Much was expected of Drew and Purdue in 2000. The Boilermakers lost a couple of heartbreakers, at Notre Dame 23-21 and at Penn State 22-20. They bounced back to upset No. 6 Michigan and No. 17 Northwestern, then rallied past Wisconsin in overtime. That set up a huge game against No. 12 Ohio State. Drew threw a bad interception in the fourth quarter that helped the Buckeyes take a 27-24 lead. But, with 2:16 left, Drew hit receiver Seth Morales, his fourth option, with a 64-yard touchdown pass to win the game.

"I'm still in shock about what happened at the end," Drew told the Lafayette, Indiana, *Journal & Courier*'s Tom Kubat.

He was even more shocked when Colts quarterback Peyton Manning called to congratulate him. It was the first time they had ever spoken. It would not be the last.

The Boilermakers went on to share the Big Ten title and earn a spot in the Rose Bowl for the first time in 34 years. They lost to No. 4 Washington, 34-24, finishing 8-4. Drew finished third in the Heisman Trophy voting. He also became an Academic All-American.

Drew was so popular, West Lafayette officials named a street, Brees Way, after him.

Despite all the attention, Drew never forgot what was important. He worked with elementary school kids. He joined the American Lung Association's anti-smoking drive called, "Enjoy the Brees, Don't Smoke."

Overall Drew set two NCAA passing records, 12 Big Ten records, and 18 school records. He was the 2000 Maxwell Award winner as the nation's outstanding college player. He was on his way to graduating with honors from Purdue's prestigious Krannert School of Management.

Next stop—the NFL.

Despite all the attention, Drew never forgot what was important.

Drew started his NFL career as a San Diego Charger.

Charging Up

Most players with NFL dreams drop out of school the second semester of their senior year to work out and prepare for the NFL draft in April. Not Drew. He stayed in school to finish his degree in industrial management (he would earn a 3.42 grade point average out of a 4.0 scale). That meant he would train alone at Purdue instead of at a facility in Bradenton, Florida, run by his agent's company, IMG. His agent, Tom Condon, wasn't happy, but Drew was determined to graduate on time.

San Diego made him the first pick of the second round in April of 2001. Drew signed a four-year deal worth $10 million. He got $1.8 million right away as a bonus.

In the San Diego media guide of 2001, Chargers coach Mike Riley called Brees "a classic gym rat." In other words, Drew did a lot of work on his own to get better. Still, the Chargers signed thirty-eight-year-old Doug Flutie because they didn't want a rookie quarterback running the offense.

Drew eventually became the starter, but after two years of inconsistency, Flutie replaced him. At that point Drew had a 10-17 record as a starter and had thrown 31 interceptions against 29 touchdown passes. San Diego officials didn't think he was the answer, so in the NFL draft of 2004 they got a highly regarded quarterback, Philip Rivers.

That motivated Drew. He hired dietitians, exercise experts, personal trainers and even a former Major League Baseball pitching coach. He went from the NFL's 29th-rated quarterback in 2003 to the Pro Bowl in 2004. The Chargers decided to keep Drew and signed him to an $8 million franchise player contract for the 2005 season.

The San Diego Chargers brought in veteran Doug Flutie (right) to show a young Drew how to become a successful NFL quarterback.

In November 2004, Brees led the Chargers to a 43-17 victory over the New Orleans Saints. He made four touchdown passes with no interceptions in that game. His stellar 2004 performance earned him an impressive 104.8 quarterback rating.

Drew had another big year, but in San Diego's last game, his shoulder was severely injured by Denver defensive tackle Gerard Warren. Drew dived for a loose ball and the 300-pound Warren smashed his shoulder, tearing the labrum and rotator cuff. Doctors weren't sure it would heal well enough for him to ever play again. The Chargers released Drew and named Philip Rivers their quarterback.

Drew would have to find another home.

Drew isn't always serious. He and his Saints teammates celebrated their Super Bowl win with a victory parade through New Orleans. Drew was also in a parade at Disney World with Mickey Mouse.

Saving Each Other

$\mathcal{D}$rew and New Orleans both seemed to be lost causes in the winter of 2006. Drew had his wrecked shoulder. New Orleans had suffered hundreds of millions of dollars in damage from Hurricane Katrina. Would either ever recover?

Many teams believed Drew's career was over. Only two of the NFL's 32 teams—Miami and New Orleans—were interested in him after the Chargers released him.

New Orleans Coach Sean Payton believed in Drew. He loved Drew's accuracy, intelligence, courage, and leadership. He had no doubt Drew would make a fine quarterback for the Saints.

The Saints' stadium, the Superdome, was a mess from Hurricane Katrina. It needed $200 million in repairs. Team officials considered leaving for San Antonio or Los Angeles, but the city and fans needed something to believe in, and a winning football team would be a huge boost. Saints officials agreed to stay until 2025. Now they needed a good team, and that meant finding a great quarterback. They decided that was Drew. Just as important, Drew decided New Orleans was the city for him.

"When I first came here it looked like a bomb had gone off," he told Joseph Guinto of *American Way*. "I got the feeling they had more confidence in me and my ability to come back from surgery than I did. That meant a lot."

He signed a six-year, $60 million contract. Still, it was always about more than money.

"People looked at New Orleans having been displaced for a year," Drew told Bob McManaman of *The Arizona Republic*, "and said, 'Hey, where are you going to live? The organization is in shambles.' But for me, when I visited New Orleans, I saw an opportunity. I felt like it was a calling for me. Not only to come here and help turn the organization around . . . but to help with the rebuilding of a city and a region.

"How many people get that opportunity in a lifetime? I felt like it was a defining moment in my life making that decision."

After their marriage in 2003, Drew and Brittany had started the Brees Dream Foundation to help advance cancer research and to help kids in need. Now they would use the foundation to help New Orleans. It raised millions of dollars to help rebuild schools and athletic fields, including a new football stadium for the Ninth Ward public schools. That generosity earned Drew the 2006 NFL Man of the Year Award. He and Brittany also donated $2 million to Purdue's academic center.

"It's the most any former Purdue athlete has ever given back to the university," Tom Schott said.

Drew's involvement with cancer research led to his friendship with Micah Roshell, a young boy from New Orleans who was battling cancer and needed two bone marrow transplants. Drew visited Micah in the hospital in January of 2010 and gave him the game ball from the Saints' playoff win over Arizona.

"Drew is a better person than a player, and he's a great player, because he was raised that way," Joe Tiller said. "He's

Drew is a big believer in helping people. He shows kids how it's done during a sports clinic in New Orleans.

a very compassionate guy. He's a caring guy who has difficulty saying no. He's kind of a sucker in that way. That's why he started his foundation. That way he can pick and choose who to help."

Drew doesn't let fame go to his head. He and his family live in a 120-year-old house in Uptown, the city's oldest neighborhood. They often take family walks with their dog, Alexis, and stop to talk with neighbors. You'd never know he was one of sports' biggest stars. Heck, he eats a peanut butter and jelly sandwich the night before every game. His favorite fast food comes from In-N-Out Burger. Before every game he puts on his socks the same way, for good luck.

No one guessed he would lead the Saints to a Super Bowl victory when he joined the team in the spring of 2006. Because his shoulder was still healing from surgery, he couldn't throw a football 10 yards. But he worked hard and was ready for the season. He made the Pro Bowl after throwing for 26 touchdowns and 4,418 yards.

In his first four seasons in New Orleans, no NFL quarterback had more completions (1,572), thrown for more yards (18,298) or passed for more touchdowns (122).

In 2008 Drew threw for 5,069 yards, missing Dan Marino's NFL record by 22 yards. A few weeks after the season ended, on January 15, 2009, Drew's son, Baylen, was born.

The stage was set for the Saints' dream 2009 regular season. They won their first 13 games. Drew threw six touchdown passes in the season opener, with Baylen watching. He led the league in touchdown passes (34) and quarterback rating (109.6). He set an NFL record for accuracy by completing 70.6 percent of his passes. He also threw for 4,388 yards. It was the fourth straight year he had thrown for more than 4,000 yards, the only person besides Peyton Manning to do so. The Saints had the NFL's best offense, averaging 31.9 points and 403.8 yards. Drew was so popular he even got to film a commercial with President Barack Obama at the White House.

Brees was even better in the 2009 playoffs. In the Saints' 45-14 opening win over Arizona he was 23-for-32 for 247 yards and three touchdowns. In the 31-28 overtime win over Minnesota he was 17-for-31 for 197 yards and three TDs.

He had done everything that everyone had ever expected of him, except win a Super Bowl championship. And then, on a humid night in Miami, he delivered that, too, and remembered how far he and New Orleans had come.

"Eighty-five percent of the city was under water, all the residents evacuated all over the country, people never knowing if they were coming back or if New Orleans would

A lot of players talk about how important their family is, but Drew lives the talk. He made sure wife Brittany and son Baylen were with him after the Saints beat the Indianapolis Colts to win Super Bowl XLIV.

come back," he said in the press conference after the Super Bowl press conference. "But not only the city came back, and the team came back . . . when the players got there, we all looked at one another and said, 'We're going to rebuild together.' "

He paused.

"I tried to imagine what this moment would be like. It's better than expected. I feel it was all meant to be. What can I say? The birth of my son, and in the first year of his life, we won a Super Bowl."

And then he couldn't stop the tears.

1979 Andrew Christopher Brees is born on January 15 in Dallas, Texas.

1986 Drew and his family move to Austin, Texas.

1995 As a junior, Drew becomes the starting quarterback for his high school team. He leads Westlake to a 12-0-1 regular season record, but hurts his knee and misses the playoffs.

1996 Drew comes back to lead Westlake to a 16-0 record and the Texas Class 5A (biggest school) state title. He throws for 31 touchdowns and 3,528 yards.

1997 Drew arrives as a freshman at Purdue. He is the backup quarterback and rarely plays.

1998 Drew becomes the starting quarterback as a sophomore. He is named Big Ten Offensive Most Valuable Player after throwing for a school-record 39 touchdowns and 3,983 yards. He leads Purdue to a 37-34 upset win over No. 4 Kansas State in the Alamo Bowl and a record of 9-3.

1999 Drew throws for 25 touchdowns and 3,909 yards and leads Purdue to the Outback Bowl and a 7-5 record.

2000 Drew leads Purdue to the Big Ten co-championship and a spot in the Rose Bowl. The Boilermakers lose to Washington 34-24 although Drew throws for two touchdowns. For the season Drew throws for 26 touchdowns and 3,668 yards. He finishes third in the Heisman Trophy voting. Purdue finishes 8-4.

2001 Drew graduates from Purdue with honors. He is drafted with the first pick of the second round by the San Diego Chargers. He doesn't play much as a rookie behind veteran Doug Flutie.

2002 Drew becomes the starting quarterback. He throws for 17 touchdowns and 3,284 yards.

2003 Drew marries college sweetheart Brittany Dudchenko in February. He throws for 11 touchdowns and 2,108 yards. The team struggles and Flutie replaces him as the starter for the final five games. He and Brittany start the Brees Dream Foundation.

2004 Drew becomes the starter again and throws for 27 touchdowns and 3,159 yards. He makes his first Pro Bowl. He is named NFL Comeback Player of the Year.

2005 Drew throws for 24 touchdowns and 3,576 yards. He hurts his right (throwing) shoulder in the last game. San Diego releases him.

CHRONOLOGY

2006 Drew becomes a free agent and signs with the New Orleans Saints for 6 years and $60 million. He throws for 26 touchdowns and 4,418 yards. He is named to the Pro Bowl and is also chosen as Walter Payton NFL Man of the Year for his charity work.

2007 Drew throws for 28 touchdowns and 4,423 yards. He leads the Saints to the NFC title game, where they lose to the Chicago Bears.

2008 Drew throws for 34 touchdowns and an NFL-leading 5,069 yards. He makes All-Pro.

2009 His son Baylen is born. Drew throws for an NFL-best 34 touchdowns, plus 4,388 yards. He sets an NFL record by completing 70.6 percent of his passes. The Saints open 13-0 and finish 13-3 in the regular season. He makes All-Pro again.

2010 Drew is named the Most Valuable Player as the Saints beat the Indianapolis Colts 31-17 in the Super Bowl.

CAREER STATS

Year	Team	G	Comp	Att	Pct	Yards	YPA	Lg	TD	Int	Rate
2009	New Orleans	15	363	514	70.6	4,388	8.54	75	34	11	109.6
2008	New Orleans	16	413	635	65	5,069	7.93	84	34	17	96.2
2007	New Orleans	16	440	652	67.5	4,423	6.78	58	28	18	89.4
2006	New Orleans	16	356	554	64.3	4,418	7.97	86	26	11	96.2
2005	San Diego	16	323	500	64.6	3,576	7.15	54	24	15	89.2
2004	San Diego	15	262	400	65.5	3,159	7.89	79	27	7	104.8
2003	San Diego	11	205	356	57.6	2,108	5.92	68	11	15	67.5
2002	San Diego	16	320	526	60.8	3,284	6.24	52	17	16	76.9
2001	San Diego	1	15	27	55.6	221	8.18	40	1	0	94.8
Total		122	2,697	4,164	64.8	30,646	7.4	86	202	110	91.9

(G=Games, Comp=Completions, Att=Attempts, Pct=Percentage, YPA=Yards per attempt, Lg=Longest pass, TD=Touchdown, Int=Interceptions, Rate=Quarterback rating)

FURTHER READING

Books

Pulditor, Seth H. *Drew Brees*. Broomall, PA: Mason Crest Publishers, 2010.

Sandler, Michael. *Drew Brees and the New Orleans Saints: Super Bowl XLIV*. New York: Bearport Publishing, 2010.

Savage, Jeff. *Drew Brees*. Minneapolis: Lerner Classroom, 2010.

Works Consulted

Author's interview with Tom Schott, Purdue University sports information director, December 14, 2009.

Author's interview with Matt Painter, Purdue University basketball coach, January 25, 2010.

Author's interview with Joe Tiller, former Purdue University football coach, January 27, 2010.

Associated Press. "Mina Brees Died of Drug Overdose." November 21, 2009.

CBSSports.com Wire Reports. "Saints Clobber Cardinals, Advance To NFC Title Game." January 16, 2010.

Corbett, Jim. "Everything But the Title: Brees Is Crashing the QB Party." *USA Today*, October 2, 2009.

Editor. "10 Hot Hoosiers." *Indianapolis Monthly*, February 1999.

Editor. "Drew Brees Regular Season Notes." *Indianapolis Star*, January 21, 2010.

Editor. "Purdue's Prodigy, QB Drew Brees." *Sports Illustrated College Football Preview*, August 16, 1999.

Editor. "Saints QB Drew Brees Named SN's Offensive Player of the Year." *The Sporting News*, January 12, 2010.

George, Thomas. "Reggie Bush Finally Speaks Softly, Carries Big Stick." *AOL FanHouse*, January 16, 2010.

Guinto, Joseph. "Drew Brees, New Orleans' Renaissance Man." *American Way*, September 1, 2007.

Holder, Larry. "Having Brees Instead of Romo Has Saints Feeling Blessed." *CBSSports.com*, December 18, 2009.

Justice, Richard. "A Saint's Mission, Drew Brees Realizes How Uplifting His Team's Success Is to the City of New Orleans, and He's Doing More than His Part On and Off the Field." *Houston Chronicle*, February 4, 2010.

Kaminiski, Kevin. "Passing Fancy—Purdue's Big Push." *Football News*, October 9, 1999.

King, Peter. "Drew Brees, the Heart of New Orleans." *Sports Illustrated*, January 18, 2010.

———. "Who Dat! Saints Strut to Their First Super Bowl." *Sports Illustrated*, February 1, 2010.

Kubat, Tom. "Chargers Grant Brees' Wish." *Journal & Courier* [Lafayette, Indiana], March 25, 2005.

———. "Time of His Life." *Journal & Courier* [Lafayette, Indiana], September 20, 2001.

Layden, Tim. "Hang Time." *Sports Illustrated*, April 30, 2001.

———. "Unshaken, Unbroken, Unbeaten." *Sports Illustrated*, November 2, 2009.

Lewis, Tim. "Student of the Game." *Krannert Magazine*, Fall 2000.

McManaman, Bob. "Drew Brees Formed Deep Bond With Big Easy." *The Arizona Republic*, January 12, 2010.

Mariotti, Jay. "Saints and Their City Finally Get a Break." *FanHouse*, January 25, 2010.

Martel, Brett. "Brees Says He Won't Let Manning Affect His Game." Associated Press, February 2, 2010.

———. "Former Purdue QB Brees Is Fan Favorite For His Work On, Off Field." Associated Press, December 19, 2009.

New Orleans Coach Sean Payton Press Conference, January 20, 2010.

Purdue Boilermakers: "Brees, Manning Make Super Bowl History." January 28, 2010.
http://www.purduesports.com/sports/m-footbl/spec-rel/012810aab.html

———. "Brees Named to Inaugural 'All-Fundamentals' Team." December 10, 2009.
http://www.purduesports.com/sports/m-footbl/spec-rel/121009aab.html

San Diego Chargers Media Guide. Chargers Public Relations Department. Neyenesch Printers, 2001.

Schott, Tom. *The History of the Boilermakers*. Purdue University Football Vault. Atlanta: Whitman Publishing LLC, 2008.

Sullivan, Tim. "Letting Go of Letting Brees Go." *San Diego Union-Tribune*, January 26, 2010.

On the Internet

Brees Dream Foundation
http://www.drewbrees.com

Drew Brees
http://www.NFL.com

Drew Brees
http://www.purduesports.com